Su
of Dalai Lama and
Desmond Tutu's
THE BOOK OF
JOY

*Lasting Happiness in a
Changing World*

by SUMOREADS

TABLE OF CONTENTS

EXECUTIVE SUMMARY

In their book *The Book of Joy: Lasting Happiness in a Changing World*, the Dalai Lama and Desmond Tutu team up with Douglas Abrams to explore the nature of joy and suffering, the source of the emotions that preclude the experience of joy, and the attributes individuals can nurture to live a fulfilling and joyful life.

The authors point out that no one ever set out to find joy and found it. Joy has to ensue, and it only ensues from an acceptance of suffering as a fact of life, from the adoption of a more accommodating perspective, from a selfless concern for the well-being of others, and from meditative practices that develop mental immunity. The authors invite the reader to embrace suffering as the crucible that refines and fills the spirit with generosity and magnanimity, the absence of which true joy would be unknown.

In the weeklong dialogues that culminate in *The Book of Joy*, the Dalai Lama and Desmond Tutu challenge anyone who wants to experience lasting joy to shelf his self and reach out to the stranger on the street and to anyone suffering, because the human race is interdependent and connected. Excessive self-focus, they argue, disconnects and alienates the individual from himself and from others and precludes the experience of joy.

DAY 1
THE NATURE OF TRUE JOY

Key Takeaway: Joy is not an escape from suffering

Fear, pain, suffering, and death are the inevitabilities of life. To discover joy is not to escape their certainty. The true value of joy is in elevating the human spirit so that it can face hardship and heartbreak with dignity and ease.

Key Takeaway: Joy grows from inside the self

The ultimate goal of any sentient being is to find happiness and avoid suffering.

Happiness is elusive and fleeting because people seek it from outside of themselves—from money, power, status, and other outward achievements. Regardless of the size or significance of an outward gain, the human mind always acclimates to the change. When this happens, it defaults to the natural state of happiness—to the state determined by the individual's internal values.

The source of a happy life, of physical health and enduring joy, is deep inside. It is in caring for the well-being of others; in nurturing compassion and generosity. Nature has wired human beings to care for and be generous to others, to thrive in community and fellowship, and to shrivel in self-centeredness and isolation.

Key Takeaway: Self-centeredness breeds suffering

Physical or sensory pain is inevitable and irrepressible. Mental pain, or suffering, is optional.

Most of the suffering people experience stems from a prolonged deficiency of kindness and compassion, the product of a disproportionate focus on materialistic values. It is the self-centeredness that pervades modern cultures that breeds the insecurity, fear, and distrust that cause so much anguish today. When you realize that you are not alone—that, by virtue of your humanity, you are connected even to the stranger on the street—and unite your suffering with the suffering of people around you or elsewhere in the world, you lessen your pain.

You diminish your suffering not when you deny its existence, but when you realize that all of humanity is connected and use this realization to nurture compassion and generosity your fellow man.

Key Takeaway: Your attitude to suffering determines who you become

Suffering, whichever form it takes, is a necessary part of life.

"There are going to be frustrations in life. The question is not: How do I escape? It is: How can I use this as something positive?" (p. 39).

Your person and character is forged in the crucible of suffering. You can perceive your suffering as a pointless and frustrating experience and become bitter, or you can choose to appreciate it as part of the pain that precedes every beautiful thing and use it to nurture humility, compassion, and forgiveness.

Even in the depth of the worst of pain, you have the freedom to look away from yourself and recognize the anguish of those who suffer as you do. You have the freedom to bear your pain with dignity and examine how an unwanted situation may help you grow and mature.

A lot of suffering comes from excessive focus on the self, and a lot of happiness comes from practicing compassionate concern for the wellbeing of others.

Key Takeaway: Lasting satisfaction comes from beyond the senses

Joy and happiness can be experienced through the senses or through the mind. The satisfaction that comes from sensory experiences, like good food, music, and sex, is temporary and fleeting. Lasting joy is experienced at a deeper, mental level through the practice of love, compassion, generosity, and spirituality.

The way to create joy is to turn to others and be a source of calm, peace, and joy for them, because joy—like love, compassion, and generosity—is contagious.

You can find lasting happiness—regardless of your external circumstances—through a genuine concern for the wellbeing of others. A few minutes of meditation on kindness and compassion for others can keep you calm and joyous throughout the day.

DAYS 2 AND 3
THE OBSTACLES TO JOY

Key Takeaway: Mental immunity is a skill you develop

The attitude you take to your circumstances and relationships creates either joy or suffering. Contemplative and spiritual practices—such as prayer, meditation, and intention-setting—adjust your attitude and help you develop immunity to the suffering created by unwanted emotions.

When you develop mental immunity, it's easier to avoid the harmful thoughts and emotions that create suffering and cultivate the emotions that bring true joy. Mental immunity does not eliminate suffering; it simply makes you less susceptible to the distress that comes with negative situations, thoughts, and feelings.

Key Takeaway: Introspection and acceptance build mental immunity

Part of building mental immunity is to ask yourself if the negative emotions you feel are based on something real or are just projections of your mind. The other part is to ask yourself if you are complicit in creating the circumstances you don't want. With consistent practice, you will realize that the judgments you make (of situations being good, bad, or neutral) and the responses you make to these judgments (unwanted emotions like frustration, fear, and anger) are biased mental projections.

People are compassionate by nature. If they upset you, it's likely a misunderstanding, an expression of their negative circumstances, or a misdirection of their destructive emotions. You can choose to reframe your frustration or anger into compassionate concern.

Negative emotions are natural. It's the thought that they are inappropriate that makes them more intense. It takes practice, with either prayer or meditation, to accept that life is full of suffering and that negative emotions are natural.

Key Takeaway: A distorted perception of reality creates fear, anxiety, and worry

Fear, like stress, evolved to keep you alert and wary of mortal danger. Fear becomes oppressive when it is exaggerated or when it arises out of trivial mishaps.

Stress and anxiety are the products of bloated expectations and ambitions, the malaise of a self-centered mind. The antidote to these emotions is a realistic perception of reality and one's abilities. A realistic perception sets the mind on realistic goals and invites one to make realistic efforts.

The connected life of a tribe throughout most of human history made fear manageable. Although there was less to eat, and although there was more loss than there is today, there wasn't as much constant pressure because expectations were modest and efforts were less focused.

Fear, anxiety, and worry—the emotions that preclude the presence of joy—emanate from chasing after ambition and time. When you realize that the settled joy you seek comes from love and connection, and that it is here and now, ambition—that materialistic desire for more—ceases to be your foremost concern.

Key Takeaway: Reframe stress and fear to build resilience

Stress is a natural response to danger. It triggers the physiological changes that enable you to fight or take flight from a threat. A constant and adverse reaction to threats—whether real or perceived, as in the fear of losing a job—wears down the DNA caps that protect cells from aging and disease.

When you reframe the stress agents you encounter every day and see them as challenges, your body responds differently. And when you think of other people, no matter how different, as pieces of the connected humanity which you are part of, they cease to be threats. It is the thought of being special or different that creates isolation and raises suspicion, fear, stress, and anxiety.

Breathing practices, meditation walks, and exercise help you observe quiet time, dial down the fight-or-flight reflex, and calm your thoughts and emotions.

Key Takeaway: Introspection abates frustration and anger

Anger is a secondary emotion, a defense mechanism that activates when you feel threatened. The fear of loss or less underlies feelings of anger. You get angry because you think you will lose what you want or because you think you are less respected or loved than you deserve. To deal with anger, you have to confront the underlying fear. Examine it, and acknowledge that you feel afraid or threatened.

When you acknowledge the role you play in creating your unwanted emotions, and when you recognize that the people creating your angst have their own human fears and hurts, you give yourself a chance to rise above your anger.

Key Takeaway: Embrace your sadness and grief to lighten your emotional load

Sadness and grief fester and grow when they are bottled up inside. Learn to cry out your sadness and shout out your pain. It's pretending these emotions are not there that maims you.

Part of joy is the acceptance of all emotions, including fear, anger, and sorrow, because they are natural and necessary emotions. Grief is a reminder of lost love, and brief sadness can be the source of empathy and generosity, a nudge to reach out for support and love.

The way to overcome the sadness and grief that come from the loss of a close friend or relative is to channel the sorrow to a greater purpose: to an ambition that would make the one you lost happy. You are less likely to sink into despair if you focus on what you have to do rather than the loss you have suffered.

Key Takeaway: A wider perspective palliates despair

The human race has a capacity for unspeakable atrocities, but it also has a capacity for unbridled goodness. It's possible to find joy in a world filled with so much crime, poverty, and wars, when you think of the human capacity for compassion—when you think, for example, of all the people who give up the comfort of their lives to reduce the pain of those ravaged by war or disease.

When you consider how far the world has come from a hundred years ago, you will realize that humanity is changing and learning to be compassionate. Focus on this change to ignite a positive attitude within yourself. Embrace the despair in the news and around you, and use it to show compassion where you are. If there's nothing you can do to help, it's enough to feel compassion, to visualize your love and forgiveness and wish it on the people who need it.

"We've always got to be recognizing that despite the aberrations, the fundamental thing about humanity, about humankind, about people, is that they are good, they were made good, and they really want to be good" (p. 120).

There are many incredibly good things happening in the world, but the media does not report them because they are too common. Don't look at the negatives in isolation; take on a wider perspective to abate the despair you feel.

Key takeaway: A warm heart is the antidote to loneliness

Although there are millions of people in most modern cities, there is little space for friendship and love, for the human connection, because people are in too deep in the incessant rush of a materialistic culture.

A competitive mind—a mind excessively self-focused and obsessed with differences or feelings of superiority—breeds fear and distrust and emotionally distances itself. When you relate to people on the human level, differences in the secondary level—in race, nationality, religion, and status—become inconsequential. Strangers, even enemies, become potential friends. An open heart, warm and full of trust, always thinking about the next person, does not feel lonely, even when the body is physically alone.

Key Takeaway: Gratitude and sympathetic joy scatter envy

Regardless of any social equality initiative rolled out, there will always be people who are more successful, who have more, and who are smarter or better-looking than you are.

Upward comparisons breed discontent and resentment—two of the destructive emotions that corrode your peace of mind, weaken your relationships, and make it impossible to experience joy.

Beating envy is a multi-fold process that begins with forgiving yourself:

• Practice acceptance. Acknowledge the guilt and self-criticism causing your envy and accept the circumstances that are beyond your control.

• Reframe your envy. Ask yourself why you need a bigger house when you have a small family, or why you need a luxury car when you could help save the environment with the smaller, electric model.

• Focus on inner values. When your greatest value is the experience of knowledge or concern over the well-being of others, you feel less envious of the material possessions of others.

• Make gratitude a daily exercise. Keep a daily list of the things you are grateful for. It takes away your focus from the things you lack.

• Practice *Mudita*/sympathetic joy. You can rejoice in the good fortune of others when you recognize that you are all part of shared humanity, with similar aspirations and fears. Imagine how happy the person you are envious of is in his good fortune and what it must mean for the people who depend on him.

Key Takeaway: Suffering and adversity make possible the experience of joy

Suffering is an opportunity to grow your inner spirit, to learn, and to become firm. It brings you closer to life and the truth because it corrodes your arrogance and forces you to confront your true self. Only through the experience of suffering can anyone grasp and appreciate true happiness.

The experience of joy is not an escape from suffering and adversity; it is a way through the hard times. You don't experience joy *in spite of* your suffering; you experience it *because* of the suffering.

It's easier to go through suffering when you realize that it is both impermanent and a vital source of learning and growth. It's easier still when you realize everyone suffers, and that your suffering is not targeted punishment.

Key Takeaway: Acceptance is the way through illness and fear of death

As with suffering and adversity, you can find meaning and growth in illness. Life-threatening illnesses and near-death experiences are invitations to reexamine your life and live more purposefully.

The way through death is to embrace it as the fact of life it is. Every life form is always changing, as is every moment. Because of its inevitability, death makes life meaningful for those who are alive. The fear of death ceases when you live more purposefully; when you commit to caring for and helping others.

Key Takeaway: Meditation slows a reactive mind

Meditation, whether through breathing exercises or prayer, frees the mind from its innate tendency to make rush decisions when the fight-or-flight mechanism kicks in. It elongates the pause between stimulus and response so that one can reflect on his options and make a deliberate rather than reactive response.

DAYS 4 AND 5
THE EIGHT PILLARS OF JOY

Key Takeaway: Joy is not something you pursue—it has to ensue

Joy ensues from the ability to have perspective, humility, humor, and acceptance and from the capacity to nurture forgiveness, gratitude, compassion, and generosity. The first four pillars of joy are qualities of the mind, the last four of the heart.

"...Joy is a by-product... If you set out and say, I want to be happy, clenching your teeth with determination, this is the quickest way of missing the bus" (p. 193).

Key Takeaway: A wider and positive perspective is the foundation of joy

The way you see the world determines the way you feel and the way you act.

Your capacity to experience joy hinges on your ability to reframe your circumstances—to find meaning and to see opportunity for growth and transformation in loss and in unwanted change. When you take on a wider perspective of your situations, you reduce your worry and anxiety and invite in joy.

To gain a wider perspective, step back, look beyond your self-interest—beyond your anger and fear—and try to see your negative situation from at least six angles. Loosen your focus

16

on the one outcome you have in mind, and consider all the good things that came from the bad of your past. Consider how insignificant the situation will be a decade from now.

Even in the absence of negative circumstances, the wide-perspective approach to life leads you to rise above the self-centeredness that hinders joy. When you consider that the person who cuts you off in traffic could be rushing his sick wife to hospital, or that there are thousands of people in the world suffering exactly as you are, you lessen your anguish and become calmer.

Key Takeaway: Humility underlies the connectedness at the heart of happiness

Everyone you meet has the same human fears and worries, the same desire to be happy, as you. You lose this perspective and miss the chance to be compassionate and connected when you consider yourself special. Humility is nothing more than the recognition that whatever role or status you have is temporary, but your identity as a connected human being, equal in value with the other seven billion sentient beings, is permanent. Everyone is born the same way, and everyone dies the same way.

When you relate to everyone you meet on the human level, you break the walls that isolate you from others and from happiness. Catch yourself judging and remind yourself that you have the same vulnerabilities and aspirations as the person you judge, and that in this way you are alike and need each other.

When you cultivate humility, you free yourself to laugh at yourself, to embrace your limitations, and accept that there is room for growth.

Key Takeaway: Humor emphasizes shared ridiculousness, shared humanity

Humor brings people to the same level, just as humility does. When people laugh, especially at themselves, they are reminded of their frailties and their shared humanity. Humor is an indication of trust—it shows that you trust the other person enough to make fun of yourself or of him without the fear of losing his good graces.

Humor is fundamental to the concept of joy because it palliates life's cruelties and uncertainties, puts people at ease, and invites them to take life less seriously, to relax and connect. When you belittle and laugh at yourself, you expose a vulnerability that gives others a peek into your human side and makes it easier to connect with you.

Humor is a skill you develop. Look for it in everyday life, and take every chance to laugh at yourself and at life.

Key Takeaway: Acceptance is the source of positive change

Only by accepting the reality of life—its beauty and imperfection, joys and suffering, and everything that happens to you—can you begin to change, to create a better world for yourself and others, and to move into joy.

Acceptance is not resignation or a passive approach to difficult situations or relationships; it's a more functional perspective from which you approach life's challenges. It's easier to change the direction of the sail when you are moving with the wind than when you are railing at its caprice.

Acceptance means loosening your attachment to your aspirations. It means committing to work hard towards a goal but realizing that the outcome is influenced by numerous factors outside your control.

When you accept that life is what is, and not what you want or expect it to be, you drop the reactions that cause most of your judgment, dissatisfaction, anxiety and stress and take on an air of ease, of comfort and contentment.

Meditative practice brings you to the present and enables you to see life more accurately and to make more skillful reactions.

Key Takeaway: Forgiveness breaks your ties to the past and heals you

Everyone is capable of forgiveness and of being forgiven.

Compassion is not reserved for the people going through acute pain and suffering; it needs to be exercised towards the people causing the suffering, as well, because they too are human. To exercise this compassion, close your eyes, visualize and try to take in the anger and fear of the people causing your pain, and then pass on to them your forgiveness and love.

Forgiveness does not mean accommodation of wrongdoing; it does not mean you will forget the wrongs made, and it does not preclude the pursuit of justice. It means separating the actor from the action and responding to the actor with compassion, and to the wrongdoing with firmness. Without forgiveness, bitterness ties you to the wrongs of the past and traps you in a void of unhappiness. Whereas bitterness and retaliation create a perpetual cycle of revenge, forgiveness breaks this cycle, creates healing, and renews relationships.

Key Takeaway: Gratitude elevates your enjoyment of life

At the core of joy is the ability to see possibility and wonder in every new experience, every encounter. Gratitude enables you to celebrate every moment before it slips away.

Gratitude is about being thankful for everything that has led you to and that is in this moment. Thankfulness overwhelms feelings of lack and creates a state of abundance, of contentment, of enjoyment, of joy.

Key Takeaway: Compassion shifts concern from the self and alleviates suffering

Your suffering lessens when you think about lessening the suffering of others. Helping others does not make your suffering go away, but it transforms your pain and makes it bearable—more bearable than when you close yourself in and agonize over your misfortune.

Compassion works because it is in human nature to care. When you do something that alleviates the suffering of others, your brain activates its reward centers and releases oxytocin—which gives you the warm feeling.

Compassion is an invitation to open your heart and to rise above your vulnerabilities, your need to compete, and your fear of being taken advantage of. It starts with self-compassion: with recognizing your shortcomings as a fallible human being, accepting the parts of yourself that you are not satisfied with, and caring for and being kind to yourself, just as you would be to someone close.

Key Takeaway: Generosity creates the space that joy fills

Generosity, which often grows from compassion, is an expression of human connectedness and interdependence. Like other pro-social behaviors, it strengthens relationships and boosts health and life expectancy. When you give, you create space to receive more.

"In fact, taking care of others, helping others, ultimately is the way to discover your own joy and to have a happy life" (p. 275).

There's an innate capacity for generosity in everyone, regardless of his or her status or ability. When you have nothing material to give, you can give your time, open your heart and give solace, or give your wisdom. You can be generous with your spirit and give patience, kindness, forgiveness, or a warm heart to the people who need these gifts the most.

If you feel overwhelmed by the all the suffering in the world, all the people you feel you need to help, start where you are and do what you can. You can't solve everything by yourself, but your generosity can catch on and make significant change.

EDITORIAL REVIEW

In the *Book of Joy*, The Dalai Lama and Desmond Tutu argue that people are most joyful when they focus on others, not on themselves, and that the fastest way to experience joy is to give it or wish it on others. The Dalai Lama, reflecting on years of meditative practice, observes that:

"Even ten minutes of meditation on the well-being of others can help one to feel joyful for the whole day— even before coffee" (p. 261).

The Dalai Lama and Archbishop Tutu view joy as the enduring state of happiness that does not depend on external circumstances. They see it as a way of being of the mind and heart, nurtured through spiritual practices that invite positive thoughts, feelings, and actions. Their understanding of joy is best captured by the words of Anthony Ray Hinton, who spent thirty years in prison for a crime he did not commit:

"The world didn't give you your joy, and the world can't take it away" (p. 245).

Douglas Abrams serves as the facilitator of the weeklong conversations that the Dalai Lama and Archbishop Tutu— who are arguably two of the world's most iconic spiritual leaders—share at the Dalai Lama's home in Dharamsala, India. He sets probing questions, expounds the Dalai Lama and Archbishop Tutu's ideas without getting in their way, and complements their wisdom with personal observations and scientific findings, the product of which is a moving and fascinating take on one of the most sought-after yet elusive aspirations—joy.

Both the Dalai Lama and Archbishop Tutu make a strong emphasis on compassion, love, and connectedness as the sources of joy. They disclose personal and moving experiences, from the Dalai Lama's flight to exile to Archbishop Tutu's struggle with prostate cancer, to highlight the value of suffering as a precursor of joy.

The bulk of *The Book of Joy* is not so much a guide to joy as it is a collection of intimate conversations that the authors hope will bring out the human side people have stifled in their materialistic and competitive cultures. Towards the end, Abrams squeezes in some quick meditative practices the reader can use to develop the mental experiences and immunity that the Dalai Lama and Archbishop Tutu view as necessary to the experience of joy. In this way, he completes what turns out to be a comprehensive and easily digestible take on joy and suffering.

ABOUT THE AUTHORS

The Dalai Lama, Tenzin Gyatso, is the 14th and the current Dalai Lama—a premier monk of the Gelug school of Tibetan Buddhism and a symbol of unity of the state of Tibet. He received the Nobel Peace Prize in 1989 for his nonviolent campaign to end China's domination of Tibet. He travels extensively speaking about the welfare of Tibetans and advocating for issues touching on Buddhism, interfaith dialogue, non-violence, and the environment, among other topics.

Desmond Mpilo Tutu is a South African social activist, co-chairman of the World Justice Project, and one of the patrons of The Forgiveness Project. He was the first black Archbishop of the Anglican Church of Southern Africa and one of the most notable religious leaders in the fight against Apartheid. He teaches love and compassion and passionately campaigns against racism, poverty, and homophobia.

Douglas Abrams is an American author, editor, and literary agent. He has coauthored Desmond Tutu's *God Has a Plan*, edited Tutu's *Made for Goodness*, and authored relationship books of his own. He is the founder and president of Idea Architects, a literary agency that leverages the power of books and media to help create a better world.

If you enjoyed this summary, please leave an honest review on Amazon.com…it'd mean a lot to us.

If you haven't already, we encourage you to purchase a copy of the original book.

Made in the USA
Columbia, SC
13 March 2023

13719246R00015